CW01661510

Explaining the Resurrection

David Pawson, MA, BSc

Sovereign World

Sovereign World Ltd
PO Box 777
Tonbridge
Kent, TN11 0ZS
United Kingdom

Series editor: Susan Cuthbert

ISBN: 1 85240 348 9

Typeset by CRB Associates, Reepham, Norfolk
Cover design by CCD, www.ccdgroup.co.uk
Printed in the United States of America

Contents

Prologue

Plato, Socrates and Aristotle
are dead.

Julius Caesar, Napoleon Bonaparte and Adolph Hitler
are dead.

Cleopatra, Boadicea and Florence Nightingale
are dead.

Leonardo da Vinci, Isaac Newton and Charles Darwin
are dead.

Confucius, Buddha and Mohammed
are dead.

Karl Marx, Sigmund Freud and Albert Einstein
are dead.

Abraham Lincoln, Winston Churchill and John Kennedy
are dead.

They were all alive and are now dead,

But Jesus was dead and
is alive for evermore!
(Revelation 1:18)

1

The essential difference

The resurrection of Jesus from the dead stands alone. It was, and is, a unique event. Nothing like it has happened to anyone else, before or since.

That is why it is both the central affirmation of faith for Christians and the greatest stumbling block for unbelievers, a source of profound comfort to some and intense irritation to others. It is difficult to remain indifferent to such a startling story.

Since the happening was unparalleled, it cannot be compared with anything else; it can only be contrasted with everything else. In particular, it needs to be distinguished from the common incidence of resuscitation in the West and the common idea of reincarnation in the East.

Western resuscitation

Increased medical knowledge has enabled a growing number of people to be brought "back to life."

Methods vary from the simple "kiss of life" (blowing into the mouth after drowning or electrocution) to sophisticated techniques (calcium injections or electrode shocks after a heart attack).

An acquaintance of mine was "ten days dead" (to quote the title of his published account). Without any discernible brain activity, his heart was kept going with a pacemaker and his lungs with a respirator. Yet he recovered.

Many, including him, recount "out-of-the-body" experiences during the time they were clinically dead. For some it brought sensations of light and tranquility; for others darkness and terror. For obvious reasons, the former receive more publicity.

It seems that death separates body and spirit, but they can be reunited, within limits. The brain is quickly damaged beyond repair when deprived of oxygen.

Few such revivals happen spontaneously; most depend on someone else taking the right action at the right time. With the spread of knowledge we can expect more to be saved from this kind of death.

There are a number of examples of people being brought back to life in the Bible. In the Old Testament, Elisha raises the son of a widow in Shunem; in the New Testament, Jesus raises the son of a widow in Nain (interestingly, less than a kilometer from Shunem). When judged by the lapse of time after decease, the outstanding case is that of Lazarus (after four days).

Of course, in these cases, recovery was usually achieved by a verbal command, requiring a "miraculous" rather than a medical explanation.

Yet neither the wonders of modern science nor those of ancient scripture can help us to understand the resurrection of Jesus. The accounts of revived people are different in one vital feature.

They all came back to life, but therefore back to *death*. They all died again. Yes, life was prolonged, but not indefinitely. The reprieve was temporary; death still had the last word.

That is because resuscitation reunites the same spirit with the same mortal body. Life continues as before, to its inexorable end. No real change has taken place. The end will still come.

This is why it is misleading to talk about Jesus coming "back to life." If that is all the resurrection is about, he would have been able to continue his ministry for a few more years, gain a few more followers and perhaps visit a few other countries, though he never showed much interest in doing so. He had made many enemies and would have had to keep out of their reach if he had wanted to see old age. Inevitably, he would die again, perhaps this time with a tomb of his own and a fitting memorial stone.

But there is no such grave, no shrine containing his remains, no record of his later decease. For he never died again.

He is still alive! And he still has that body in which he met his disciples again, ate fish with them and cooked breakfast for them. Even after two thousand years, his body is still in its prime.

Fifteen hundred million people believe this incredible claim. They expect to see this body when he returns to Earth, as he promised to do. They even look forward to getting similar bodies themselves when he returns.

Such extraordinary hopes must have a remarkable source. Their roots are to be found in an empty tomb and a series of encounters which together convinced the beholders that Jesus had not only survived death, but surmounted it.

A new mode of existence had been inaugurated, in which aging, dying and putrefying had no place. Death itself was as good as dead. Eternal life was now a part of history.

Something entirely new had come into being. That is an act of creation – in fact, the act of a Creator. God himself had been busy in the darkness of a sealed and guarded grave. Nothing comparable had happened since Adam came to be and the work of making the universe had ended.

But we are rushing ahead. Just how ordinary people came to believe such extraordinary things will become apparent as we study the records of the original eye-witnesses.

One thing is clear – resurrection is about being re-embodied. Other resuscitations bring people *back* to life in their old bodies, only to eventually die again. For Jesus alone, resurrection meant going *on* to life, in a new body, never to die again.

However, this concept of living again in a new body must not be confused with the notion of reincarnation, which has become increasingly popular.

Eastern reincarnation

There is an ancient belief that after death we are born again in another body – and again and again. Each re-embodiment is determined by how we have lived in the previous existence. Thus, we may "ascend" the social scale or "descend," even to the level of animals. Who or what we return as is the result of our choices.

The resemblance of this to resurrection is only superficial. There are some radical differences.

First, the re-incarnate expect to die again. In fact, they expect to go through this disintegrating experience repeatedly. Second, the successive bodies bear no resemblance to each other, causing a crisis of identity, especially in the absence of conscious memory. "Who am I?" becomes "Who was I?" Third, the ultimate goal is to escape from a body altogether, to achieve an impersonal (and unconscious) state of existence outside time and space.

We can note two practical observations. Whereas resuscitations are established facts, reincarnation is only a theory, with no objective evidence and only highly suspect subjective claims to support it.

If the resurrection of Jesus can be established, belief in reincarnation must be abandoned. If his past is the model for our future, we retain our present identity, recognizably re-embodied, and remain in that condition for all eternity.

So, the resurrection of Jesus was unique, quite different from other concepts of life after death, but was it totally unrelated to everything that went before?

While there was no actual historical precedent for this exceptional event, it was not altogether unexpected. There were already people in the world who believed that such a thing could happen – and would.

Jesus was and is a Jew. He cannot be separated from his people, Israel. Resurrection is a Hebrew concept, which could have only grown out of the Jewish understanding of life and death, which was in marked contrast to other viewpoints, especially that of the Greek world.

2

The historical precedence

It is the misfortune of Western society to have been more influenced by Greek than Hebrew culture. This can be demonstrated in many aspects of life, including politics, architecture and sport.

One result is that like the Greeks, we are not good at "getting things together." We tend to accept their divisions into sacred and secular, eternal and temporal, spiritual and physical – usually to the detriment of the latter in each case. Flesh and spirit were considered incompatible, almost synonymous with evil and good. The body could be indulged, idolized or ignored.

By contrast, Hebrew thought began with the understanding that God created the physical world and therefore it was basically good. Physical and spiritual are interconnected; indeed they belong together, for eternity as well as time. The body is essential to being.

The difference comes out very clearly in their respective attitudes to life and death.

Greek: Immortal souls

Human beings, according to the Greek view, are basically immortal souls imprisoned within mortal bodies. This restricts our development and we cannot realize our full potential until we are liberated from our physical mortality. This can partly be achieved in this life by treating the body with contempt, either in a disciplined or dissolute manner. However, it is death that brings total and final release.

Death is therefore considered a friend to be welcomed. Socrates talked of it with eager anticipation as he drank the poison hemlock in the presence of his students. People who commit suicide still mistakenly see it as a "way out" of their troubles.

To Greeks the idea of re-embodiment after death is ridiculous, which is why some mocked Paul when he preached it on Mars Hill (Acts 17:32). Indeed, the prospect would be abhorrent, akin to imprisonment. The sooner we get rid of the body, thought the Greeks, the better.

So death was seen as a natural event, a release, and a friend to be welcomed. However, nothing could be further from Hebrew thought.

Hebrew: Resurrected bodies

To a Jew, life is a supernatural act of creation. When God created Adam, he first made a body, then breathed life into it. The phrase *"living soul"* or *"living being"* simply means "animated body"; it can be equally used of animals and humans (Genesis 1:24; 2:7). The international distress call "SOS" (Save Our Souls) is a plea to keep the body alive.

When God made human bodies, male and female, he pronounced his work *"very good,"* better than all the other *"good"* things he had brought into being. Flesh is therefore inherently good, not evil.

But flesh was not inherently immortal. The source of everlasting life has always been external to human nature, and that's why the tree of life was in the garden of Eden.

Human beings are a body-soul unity. The soul is to the body what music is to the piano: the instrument comes alive in the hands of the maestro. This understanding integrates the physical and the spiritual, the temporal and the eternal.

Life is a blessing, and by the same token, death is a curse.

To a Jew, death is a supernatural act of destruction. It need never have happened. It was a judgment, a punishment for rebellion against God's rule. Having taken the forbidden fruit of the tree of *"knowledge"* (in other words, personal experience) of good *and* evil, Adam and Eve and all their descendants have been cut off from the tree of life, their source of continued existence. Death has reigned over the human race ever since (Romans 5:17).

However, death meant an unnatural separation of body and spirit, after which the body decayed and ultimately returned to the earth from which it originally came.

But the disembodied spirit continued to exist in a shadowy underworld (called "Sheol" in Hebrew and "Hades" in Greek). Robbed of physical senses, unable to speak, the inhabitants were more "asleep" than awake.

Yet it was not oblivion. They could be awakened and appear, even speak as "ghosts." When Saul consulted the witch of Endor, she conjured up the *"spirit"* of the prophet Samuel (1 Samuel 28:11f), although such communication through mediums with the dead was strictly forbidden (Deuteronomy 18:11; Leviticus 19:31; 20:6).

With such a future prospect, it is not surprising that premature death was seen as a tragedy, while long life was considered a great blessing. Healing delivered a person from Sheol, for which God deserved special thanks (Psalm 103:4).

The miracle of resurrection from the dead was a single instance of God's mercy. Both Elijah and Elisha performed this feat, significantly with children whose life had been cut short.

Jesus compared his own *"three days and three nights"* in the tomb with the story of Jonah inside the *"great fish"* (Matthew 12:40–41). There is reason to believe that after Jonah was thrown overboard as a sacrifice to avert the wrath of God, he actually died and was brought back to life (Jonah 2:2, 6–7). In this case his would be the most outstanding "resurrection" in the Old Testament.

To escape death altogether was a supreme blessing, as the Hebrews saw it. This happened to Enoch who went for such a long walk with God that he walked right into heaven (Genesis 5:24; Hebrews 11:5). It also happened to Elijah, who was taken to heaven in a chariot (2 Kings 2:11).

So the Hebrew view of death was as negative as the Greek was positive. After death, life was restricted without the body rather than released from the body. Indeed, it could hardly be called "life" at all; it was mere existence – and therefore to be postponed as long as possible.

Yet there were glimmers of hope that personal fellowship with God could be enjoyed beyond the grave (e.g. Job 19:25–27; Psalm 73:23–26) and even that he could rescue a "soul" from Sheol (e.g. Psalm 49:15). This would particularly apply to the Holy One (Psalm 16:10f): since putrefaction is the result of sin, the holy person would be plucked from the grave before decay set in.

The concept of resurrection with a new body probably grew out of the Jews' experience of death and resurrection as a nation. As a people, they were as good as dead and buried. Yet they believed God could and would raise them up again. The prophet Hosea had already expressed this hope, using the words: *"on the third day he will restore us"* (Hosea 6:1–2).

Ezekiel's vision of the valley of *"dry bones"* was about the revival of the nation that God will bring about. But a nation is made up of individuals and Ezekiel saw them being put together again.

It is significant that Daniel, not long after, was predicting a day of general resurrection for *"multitudes"* of people (Daniel 12:2; note that it will be followed by division between two destinies). But he was only echoing what Isaiah had said much earlier (Isaiah 26:19).

After the Jews' return from Babylon, resurrection of the individual was much debated. By the time Jesus was born, the lines had been drawn between the liberal Sadducees, who were utterly skeptical about the whole idea (see their challenge to Jesus in Luke 20:27–38) and the conservative Pharisees, with whom Martha and Paul agreed (John 11:24; Acts 24:15).

But the latter had no proof of their belief that one day the dead would be raised with new bodies – other than God's Word. God had not yet done this for a single soul. Some had been resuscitated, but they had all died again. None had defeated the last enemy.

Yet they firmly believed that a day would come when God would defeat all their enemies and establish his rule in the earth. A new age would dawn, a new world would come. The kingdom of heaven would be re-established on earth.

And death would be no more.

3

The actual sequence

A hundred years ago it was fashionable to question whether Jesus ever existed. Since then many references to him have been discovered outside the Bible. Few today seriously doubt the basic facts of his life and death, as recorded in the four gospels.

He was born at Bethlehem in or before 4 BC, the year in which Herod the Great died. Given the name "Jesus" (Hebrew *Yeshua*) which means "God saves," he was brought up in Nazareth, where his father was a carpenter. Of the first thirty years of his life we know nothing, except for one glimpse at the age of twelve, when he revealed an unusual interest in the things of God.

Jesus' body developed from babyhood through boyhood to manhood. He had the normal physical experiences of being hungry, thirsty and tired. We mention this because there later arose a heretical belief called Docetism that his humanity was unreal, a phantom appearance (1 John 4:1–3). Yet he was a real embodied human being, in the flesh, "incarnate."

At the age of thirty, Jesus switched from the family business to a traveling ministry. After baptism by his cousin John and six weeks alone in the desert, he began preaching messages and performing miracles. His many followers were astonished at both.

However he made enemies as well as friends, particularly among the religious leaders, and on more than one occasion escaped with his life. He withdrew from public appearances and concentrated on the training of a small band of followers to continue his work after he was gone.

This was to happen much sooner than expected. After just three years, he was arrested, tried, found guilty and condemned to execution. This was carried out by the Roman authorities, who crucified him. A sympathetic member of the court gave the body a proper burial in his own tomb.

Such are the bare facts of his brief life, which are generally accepted today. Most people will admit that Jesus' words and deeds have had a wider influence on subsequent history than those of any of his contemporaries – though they are hard put to say why. His own followers would not be surprised. Even before his death, they had come to believe that though Jesus was certainly a real human being, he was a very remarkable one.

For a start, there were the miracles: healing the sick, enabling the lame to walk, the deaf to hear, the blind to see and the dumb to talk – and curing incurable leprosy. But controlling the wind and the waves was more divine than human (Mark 4:41), as was his claim to forgive all sins (Mark 2:10).

Somehow Jesus didn't fit the normal categories of life in this world. He seemed to belong to another world, to have come here from there, to have decided to come, to have chosen to be born!

After two and a half years with him, Peter finally blurted out what they had begun to suspect, *"You are the Christ, the Son of the living God"* (Matthew 16:16).

Immediately after this great confession, the three closest companions of Jesus were given a brief glimpse of that other world. Above the snowline on Mount Hermon, they saw Jesus with Moses and Elijah, who had been dead for centuries. They were discussing the *"departure"* which he would shortly bring to fulfillment in Jerusalem (Luke 9:31). The word used (literally *"exodus"*) could mean a death or an act of liberation, or both!

From that time on, Jesus frequently foretold his death, burial – and his resurrection. His predictions went into considerable detail. It would all happen in Jerusalem, to which he now set his face to go. He would be crucified, after suffering other torments. The Jewish authorities would be responsible, though the Gentiles would be the executioners.

The most outstanding incident on the journey was the raising of Lazarus from the dead. Jesus had brought others back to life after a few hours, but in this case the man had been in the grave four days and putrefaction must have set in. Yet the corpse was both restored and revived, though the grave cloths had to be unloosed before he could move.

Martha, the sister, had already said she believed her brother would rise again in the distant future, but Jesus' response: *"I am the resurrection and the life"* (John 11:25) is a claim to be the divine person who would raise the dead then and could do it now! He then proceeded to substantiate his claim. The resulting acclaim was to precipitate his arrest (John 11:45–53).

This event should have convinced his disciples that the powers of life and death were in Jesus' hands. He had now proved that with others; now he would have to do it for himself. He told them quite clearly that no one would take his life from him; he would voluntarily lay it down himself – and freely take it up again (John 10:17–18).

The events that followed drove all this out of their minds. Within the space of a week their hopes (and emotions) were lifted higher than ever, then dashed to the ground. The arrival of Jesus was greeted with wild enthusiasm by a huge crowd who thought their day of political freedom had come (*Hosanna* means *"save us now"*); but they felt badly let down when he whipped Jews out of the temple instead of Roman soldiers out of the fortress Antonia next door.

Within days, Jesus had been betrayed, arrested, given a hasty and illegal trial, mocked, flogged and sentenced to the most painful and prolonged death ever devised: crucifixion. To achieve this, the Jewish court, finding him guilty of the capital crime of blasphemy (claiming to be the Son of God), had to change the charge to treason (claiming to be the king of the Jews), since Roman law did not cover blasphemy.

Description of his death

Though thousands died on crosses at that time and in that place, we have a more detailed record of Jesus' crucifixion than any other. All four Gospels devote major attention to his last hours, as if these were more important than anything else.

Death by crucifixion is normally very slow, taking from two to seven days, depending on the physical condition of the victim. When the leg muscles have weakened, the body slumps and asphyxiation swiftly follows. This excruciating climax can be brought forward at any time by breaking the legs.

The surprise is that Jesus died after only six hours; and at the very time when thousands of Passover lambs were slaughtered (Exodus 12:6, cf. 1 Corinthians 5:7). His legs were not broken, as with the others. But to make quite sure that he was really dead, the Roman soldier with that responsibility thrust a spear up under the ribcage to the heart. An eye-witness observed a gush of blood and water, the symptom of a ruptured pericardium (a "broken heart").

Duration of his burial

Had Jesus not really been dead, his body would never have been released by his enemies or buried by his friends. Indeed, he would not have been buried at all if Joseph of Arimathea had not generously offered a private vault in his own garden. Crucified corpses were usually thrown into Gehenna, the deep valley south of the city which was its garbage dump (and frequently used by Jesus as a picture of hell).

The funeral was hurried. In less than three hours the Sabbath began, so there was no time to anoint the body with aromatic spices (to delay and disguise the process of decay); that would have to be done later. The head and the body were separately wound with linen, the corpse laid on its rock bed, and a heavy stone was rolled over the entrance. The next day soldiers sealed the tomb and settled down to guard it for the next few days. The authorities ordered these precautions because of Jesus' predictions about rising again. They did not believe he would, but wanted to make sure no one could fake it by removing the body (Matthew 27:62–66).

There is a discrepancy between the accounts of Jesus' promise to return from the grave. On the one hand, he said it would happen *"on the third day,"* yet he also said he would be *"three days and three nights"* in the tomb. Both cannot be right. Furthermore, it is quite impossible to fit it all in between Friday afternoon and Sunday morning!

The fact is, nobody is certain on what day he died. It was the day before a Sabbath, which has led to the widespread tradition that the crucifixion was on a Friday. Few seem to have noticed that it was not the weekly Sabbath (i.e. Saturday), but a special Sabbath to mark the beginning of the Passover feast (Leviticus 23:7; John 19:31). Like the modern Christmas, this could be any day of the week.

If Jesus died at 3pm on the Wednesday and rose again between 6pm and midnight on Saturday, everything would fit perfectly. By Jewish reckoning (which counts days from 6pm to 6pm), he would be *"three days and three nights"* in the grave. But by Roman reckoning (which counts days from midnight) he would rise *"on the third day."* We need to remember that what we would call Saturday evening was to the Jews the first day of the week (Genesis 1:2–5). Certainly, the tomb was empty well before dawn (John 20:1).

We are sure that he rose from the dead on the first day of the week, what we call Sunday and regard as a holiday, but which for the Jews (and God) is the first working day. The profound significance of this timing will be explored in a later chapter.

Meanwhile, we must ask how his friends were convinced he had indeed risen. What exactly happened on that day of all days?

4

The initial evidence

For the events of the first Easter Sunday we are of course dependent on the eyewitness accounts in the four Gospels: Matthew 28, Mark 16, Luke 24, John 20–21. It is good to study them and form one's own impression before reading the comments of others.

One thing is immediately obvious – there are apparent discrepancies of detail. Many have attempted to harmonize the four accounts in one consecutive narrative. It is difficult, though not impossible, to synchronize them.

Far from undermining the truthfulness of the testimonies, these differences actually underline it. They are exactly the kind of discrepancy expected of independent witnesses. Perfect agreement raises suspicions of a conspiracy to deceive, as is well known in every court of law.

It is all the more impressive that there is agreement on the basic events, both in order and content. The stories "fit together."

For example, all the gospel witnesses agree that the evidence for the resurrection was given before any appearances. And all agree that the first indications that something extraordinary had taken place were given to the women before the men.

In both these particulars, a divine wisdom may be discerned. The disciples were gradually prepared for the staggering revelation.

Outside the tomb

Whether it was before, during or after sunrise when the women arrived at the tomb is not totally clear. Certainly it was very early in the morning.

If Jesus' body had already been three days and three nights in the tomb, there was extreme urgency in the task of anointing it. The women may have been somewhat apprehensive about its condition. They had come at the earliest opportunity.

But if Jesus died on a Wednesday, why could they not have come on Friday morning, between the special Sabbath on Thursday and the normal Sabbath on Saturday? They must have known that soldiers had been posted to guard the tomb *"until the third day"* (i.e. Saturday; Matthew 27:64) and would have let no one in.

The women expected the guard to have been removed, which raised another problem. Who would break the seal and roll away the stone for them? It would weigh at least two tons and require a body of men to shift it (one manuscript of Mark 16:4 reads: *"a stone which twenty men could not roll away"*). It seems they only thought about this when approaching the garden, so they didn't go back for the men but went on, no doubt hoping to enlist the aid of others on their way to work.

The soldiers had indeed gone, but not because they had completed their duty. They had, in fact, deserted when an earthquake, followed by a ghostly apparition, had terrified them. The other-worldly figure, dazzling white at dead of night, had single-handedly rolled the stone away, pushed it over and sat on it, as if defying anyone to put it back. The guards fled, but were bribed to confess having fallen asleep on duty (the cost must have been high since that was a capital offence!) and woken to find the tomb broken and the body taken – supposedly by the disciples in order to perpetrate a fraudulent resurrection. This "explanation" persisted for centuries in Jewish circles.

The first surprise for the women was the rolled stone, not the absent soldiers. There would be no need for help. The entrance was wide open.

Before they could go in, they also encountered the "angel" who had rolled the stone away. Here again, there are slight discrepancies as to what actually occurred. Was there one angel or were there two? Did the encounter take place outside or inside the tomb? The differences are resolved if one angel met them outside and invited them inside where another was already seated.

They spoke to the speechless women, beginning with a mild rebuke: *"You've come to the wrong place!"* It was the right tomb, probably the only one in that private garden. But it was a place for the dead. Jesus was alive: he would be found among the living now (Luke 24:5).

The women were invited to *"come and see"* (Matthew 28:6) for themselves that there was no trace of the body they had laid there a few days before. Then they were commanded to *"go and tell"* (Matthew 28:10; Mark 16:7) the disciples what they had seen and heard.

They must be sure to tell Peter. In spite of his cowardice in denying his connection with Jesus, he was already being singled out and would be commissioned for pastoral leadership of the Church. There was also a promise that Jesus would meet them in Galilee, where the first call to follow him was accepted.

Inside the tomb

One thing was quite clear to the surprised and bewildered women. The body had gone. That was patently obvious, even in the dim light of the tomb.

It is clear that they did not examine the tomb very carefully. Like the soldiers, they fled from the scene, trembling and terrified.

In a state of shock, they could not at first deliver the message they had been given for the other disciples. It was Mary of Magdala who said she had been to the tomb alone, seen the stone rolled away and the body gone. But there had been no angelic messenger or message. She therefore assumed and reported to Peter and John that grave robbers had taken the corpse (John 20:2).

The two disciples ran to the tomb, while Mary followed with a heavy heart. John got there first, looked in and was taken aback to see the grave-clothes still there. He, too, stopped short at the sight of the body shroud and head "turban." They were still rolled up! They had simply collapsed with nothing inside them.

It was at that moment that John *"believed"* (John 20:8). The body had not been stolen – it would have been impossible to remove the body without disturbing the cloths with which it had been bound. No person could be responsible for what had taken place. Nor could any natural process of decay reduce a body to nothing so quickly.

They were looking at the effects of a divine intervention. God himself had been active in the silent tomb. A miracle had taken place.

Just how far John's faith could go at that moment, we do not know. We are told that the other disciples did not, could not, would not believe the report of the other women when they overcame their shock and broke their silence.

Women were not allowed to be witnesses in a Jewish court. Yet they were the first witnesses of the resurrection, perhaps because of their readiness to believe, as well as being the first to come to the tomb.

None of the evidence actually *proved* to the disciples that Jesus had risen from the dead, but all of it *prepared* them to believe it. Their minds had been prized open to consider an incredible possibility.

They were convinced by part of the angelic announcement: *"he is not here"*; but they were not yet sure that *"he is risen."* They knew where he was not, but they didn't know where he was. The situation was well described later that day by two travelers on the road to Emmaus: *"some of our companions went to the tomb and found it just as the women had said, but him they did not see"* (Luke 24:24). It is delightfully ironic that they said this to Jesus himself, without recognizing him!

The evidence was followed by the appearance. The proofs of his absence were followed by the proofs of his presence. Only then did they fully believe that he had been raised from the dead.

That is still the case today. Though the circumstantial evidence for the resurrection is strong enough to convince any jury, it is the experience of a personal encounter with Jesus that finally persuades people to believe that he is alive. But both the objective evidence and the subjective experience play their part in a firm faith. They confirm and strengthen each other.

5

The personal appearance

When studying the scriptural record of the personal appearance of Christ to the disciples, we need to add another source: Paul's letter to the Corinthians, chapter 15. If some members of the church in Corinth had not had problems accepting the resurrection of the body (almost certainly because of their Greek background), we might never have had this unique statement before the Gospels were penned and only a few years after the event. It includes the information that most of the eye-witnesses were still alive at the time, a confident claim that could have easily been checked by his readers.

We shall begin with this unique document. Paul's purpose in writing was to remind his readers how well-attested the resurrection had been, so he limits himself to the question of who saw him alive after his death and burial, the three events together constituting the fundamental facts of the faith (1 Corinthians 15:3–4).

Peter is first on the list. Perhaps it was on this occasion that Peter learned that Jesus had neither been unconscious nor inactive between his death and resurrection; he had been preaching the gospel to all those who were drowned in the flood of Noah's time (for this unexpected information see 1 Peter 3:18; 4:6).

The *"Twelve"* came next. Actually, it was eleven, after Judas committed suicide (in Gehenna, where the body of Jesus might have finished up).

Paul records that Jesus appeared to a large crowd of five hundred. It's possible that Matthew also refers to this occasion on a mountain in Galilee (Matthew 28:17; though he mentioned only the eleven disciples, he also said *"some doubted,"* which must imply a large number of others present).

Paul claimed that the majority of this group was available to confirm the event, though a few had died since it took place.

James, the half brother of Jesus himself, did not believe in him before his death (John 7:5). But this personal appearance completely converted him and he became both the presiding elder of the early Church and the writer of a letter in our New Testament.

Who are *"all the apostles"* and why did this appearance come after the others? Clearly it was not just the Twelve, though they may have been included. Nor was it the large crowd of hundreds, already mentioned. We need to remember that others were *"sent out"* (the Greek verb *apostellein* means just that); at one time there were seventy or so (Luke 10:1). These may have gathered together to discuss the rumors of his resurrection and some of them may have been among the one hundred and twenty who experienced the outpouring of the Holy Spirit on the day of Pentecost.

Finally Paul claimed that the very last appearance of Jesus was to himself, making him one of the *"apostles"* (1 Corinthians 9:1). However, this encounter was quite different from the others. Since it took place after Jesus ascended to heaven and regained his glory (John 17:5), his body was too bright to see clearly and Paul was blinded, as when one looks directly at the sun. This was no vague, subjective vision: Paul's companions saw the light and heard the voice, though only he made out the exact words. After identifying himself, Jesus commissioned this former persecutor of Christians to be the apostle to the Gentiles. Significantly the encounter took place on Gentile soil, beyond the border of the "holy land" of Israel.

This passage alone would be sufficient to establish that Jesus *"showed himself to them and gave many convincing proofs that he was alive"* to quote Dr. Luke's second volume (Acts 1:3). But its testimony is strengthened when supplemented by the additional information from the Gospels.

Where did the appearances occur? Matthew and Mark say Galilee; Luke says it was in and around Jerusalem. The Gospel of John says it was both. After all, the appearances took place over a period of six weeks, which allows ample time for travel between the two localities, which are less than 100 kilometers apart. It is entirely fitting that Jesus would use both geographical centers of his earlier ministry. However, note that he was never in two places at the same time, which is impossible for an embodied spirit, whether before death or after resurrection.

Jerusalem: Evening indoors

Jesus gave his disciples time to digest the possibility indicated by the empty tomb, time to prepare themselves for the shock of seeing him again. So it was quite late on that first Easter Sunday when he joined them for supper. And this timing was repeated the following Sunday. His meetings with his disciples in Jerusalem seem to have been mostly indoors and in the evening.

But there had been a few earlier appearances on that memorable day. The very first had been to a group of women as they fled from the tomb. Their fear was mixed with joy – they hardly dared believe what they had heard, but deep down they knew it must be true. Suddenly they stopped dead in their tracks. Jesus stood right in front of them. They rushed to clasp his feet and heard his oft-repeated admonition: *"Don't be afraid,"* after which he repeated the angelic message. They intuitively leapt to the truth, and did something that no Jew would dream of doing to a mere human being – they *"worshiped him"* (Matthew 28:9).

Mary of Magdala had hung around the tomb after Peter and John had left, hoping to find someone who had seen the body taken away. The corpse was still *"him"* to her, not an inanimate "it." Even the consolation of knowing where he was had been taken from her (the relatives of any missing body will understand her anguish).

Mary's meeting with Jesus can hardly have been chance; he wanted her to find him. Yet she thought he was the gardener! She was not the only one who failed to recognize him immediately, which may indicate some difference in appearance (there certainly would be change from the bloody and broken frame taken off the cross). But the voice was the same: one word, her name, was enough.

John records Jesus saying to Mary, *"Do not hold on to me"* (John 20:17). Jesus did not forbid her to touch him, as if his body was sacrosanct or ethereal; later he would invite others to handle him. The continuous present imperative with a negative means, *"Don't go on touching me."* He was telling her that she could not cling to his live body, as she had wanted to keep his dead body. He was not back to stay.

The account of Jesus' walk to Emmaus in Luke 24:13–35 is a beautiful one to ponder. The two *"disciples"* who took that famous walk were not from the inner circle of the Twelve. One was called Cleopas, perhaps the same as Clopas, the brother of Joseph, and therefore uncle to Jesus. They also failed to recognize the "stranger" who joined them on their journey. Luke writes that they *"were kept from recognizing him"* (Luke 24:16).

It was the custom at supper to ask the guest to break the loaf and distribute it. Perhaps it was they recognized him then because it was the first time they had looked at his hands – and saw the nail-prints.

No wonder they hurried back uphill to the city, even though it was now dark. They could not wait to tell the good news to the grieving disciples. But these had already heard about two other visitations – to the women and to Simon (Peter). And even while the excited newcomers told their own story, Jesus himself was there again, with his familiar greeting, *"Peace be with you"* – *Shalom* (Luke 24:36).

The records are honest enough to say that the nine who had not yet seen him could not believe their own eyes. They were sure he was an apparition, the visible but ethereal image that a disembodied spirit can assume. He showed them the marks of crucifixion in his hands and feet. He invited them to feel his *"flesh and bones,"* an invitation which no ghost could or would make – and which they declined! Only when he had taken and eaten some of their fish did they accept that he was really there among them. Not for the first or last time, he chided such reluctant and hesitant faith.

The other recorded appearance in Jerusalem was to Thomas, in the presence of the others, a week later, in the same room. He had missed out on that first day; perhaps brooding alone over his grief. When he returned to the others, he could not be persuaded that they had experienced anything more than hallucinations or, at the very most, an apparition. He demanded physical proof, tangible evidence of a real body before he could believe in a resurrection.

On the next "first day of the week," he was present. Jesus was suddenly there again, inviting Thomas to explore his wounds. Thomas never did. The fact that Jesus had known exactly what he had said to the others was proof enough for him and he confessed his faith immediately: *"my Lord and my God."* Others had called Jesus *"the Son of God."* Thomas was the first to call this carpenter from Nazareth *"God,"* without any qualification. In Jewish eyes he was committing the same blasphemy for which Jesus had been put to death. But he now knew it was the truth. The others had not believed when they saw Jesus, but so-called "doubting" Thomas did, immediately. Nevertheless, he did not have the blessing given to those who believe the testimony of others without seeing him themselves (John 20:29) – now numbering millions!

Such were the appearances of Jesus in and around the city where he had been killed and buried. But there were others in the north, around the sea of Galilee, where so much of his ministry had been exercised and so many of his followers had lived.

Galilee: Morning outdoors

There is a different atmosphere up here, as the crowded city gives way to open country. The appearances happen in broad daylight and fresh air – not the usual conditions for manifestation of spirits.

The disciples had obeyed Jesus' command to journey north and wait for him in Galilee. Typically, Peter tired of waiting and decided to fill in time by going back to fishing. Others followed his lead. After a fruitless night, they might not have been very pleased to be told by someone on the shore that he was approaching his task the wrong way. Perhaps with pessimistic skepticism, they obeyed the bystander's instructions, cast their net on the other side – and caught "153" fish. This number simply means "a lot of fish," far more than usual from one cast of the net. The whole incident was reminiscent of a similar miracle of Jesus on this very lake a few years before (Luke 5:4–10).

John realized that their advisor was Jesus, come to meet them in Galilee, as he and the angels had said. As soon as Peter heard this he grabbed his cloak and plunged into the water, swimming the 90 meters to shore, while others brought the boat and catch. To their surprise, Jesus had lit a fire and prepared a breakfast of cooked fish and bread.

There followed a traumatic but tender interview between Jesus and Peter. The fisherman looked into the charcoal fire and remembered another; while warming his hands in Caiaphas' courtyard on the fatal night when Jesus had been arrested, Peter had three times denied any connection between them. Now the memory of that cowardice was cleansed by a threefold question, about Peter's love rather than his loyalty. Then, the man who had been called on that very shore to be a fisher of people was commissioned to be a shepherd of God's people.

The other Galilee appearance is recorded in Matthew (28:16–20), this time up a mountain, where Jesus gave his hearers their marching orders for a world-wide mission, promising to stay with them until the end of the age.

Jesus had not just survived death. He had actually conquered the "last enemy." He had kept his word: *"I lay it* [my life] *down and I take it up again"* (John 10:18). He had been in total control of every situation he had faced in life; now he had proved the same in death. It took little more faith to believe that *"all authority in heaven and on earth"* had been given to him (Matthew 28:18).

6

The transitional permanence

The title of this chapter is a deliberate contradiction. There is a paradox at the heart of the resurrection. Had Jesus come back to stay?

The answer is: yes and no! He promised to be with them to the end of history, yet he left them again after just six weeks. To have him back, alive and well, must have been the most wonderful time in the disciples' lives. It lifted them from the depths of despair to the heights of joy. But what would happen now?

Would Jesus pick up the threads where he had left off, returning to his public ministry of preaching and healing? The angel's mention of *"Galilee"* might suggest that. Alternatively, would Jesus leave the country and start again elsewhere, hoping for a better response?

We know they hoped he would bring political freedom to his people, by expelling the Romans and taking the throne himself. This was a key part of the Jewish dream: they believed the Messiah, when he came, would reign, as his forefather David had done.

The crowd that welcomed him when he rode into the city was bitterly disappointed, even disillusioned. That is why they preferred a guerilla fighter to be set free rather than Jesus. The two on the road to Emmaus expressed the same disillusionment: *"we had hoped that he was the one who was going to redeem* [i.e. *liberate*] *Israel"* (Luke 24:21).

The very last question the disciples asked Jesus was the same issue: *"Lord, are you at this time going to restore the kingdom to Israel?"* (Acts 1:6). Significantly, he did not question the question, as he often did when they were based on wrong assumptions. He accepted all four premises built into their query – that

Israel once had the kingdom, had lost it, would get it back again and Jesus was the one who would do it. He only dealt with *when* this would happen and told them his Father had already fixed the date – but this was not to be shared with them. They had a very different task ahead of them, for which he had been preparing them.

In fact, Jesus did nothing public after his resurrection, much less anything political. He spent the time with his disciples, training them to be apostles. One of the major lessons they now had to learn was that their relationship with him was to be very different from before, though amazingly, it would be even better.

We can best understand how wisely he taught them this by looking again at his appearances among them. There were two aspects to each meeting.

Proofs of his presence

Jesus gave them all the evidence they could possibly need to be convinced that he really was back with them. Luke simply said *"many convincing proofs"* (Acts 1:4).

Jesus had a real body, which was visible to their sight, audible to their hearing and tangible to their touch. He allowed and invited them to handle his *"flesh and bones."* He broke bread, ate fish and cooked breakfast. He showed them the scars in his wounded hands and feet.

In this interaction with human beings and their environment, Jesus demonstrated that he had returned to this world and could be part of it. He was not a phantom apparition from another world.

Preparation for his absence

The first hint that he would be leaving this world was given to Mary of Magdala, when he told her to stop clinging to him, *"for I have not yet returned to the Father. Go instead to my brothers and tell them: I am returning to my Father and your Father, to my God and your God"* (John 20:17). She couldn't keep him, so she must not try.

The appearances were all sudden and unexpected. They never knew when he would be there. It was as if he deliberately set out to surprise them.

Nor did Jesus ever stay for long. His disappearances were also sudden and unexpected, as if he wanted to surprise them in this too.

Jesus' coming and going in this way must have led to questions in their minds. Apart from surprising them, what was he trying to do? Where was he spending most of his time? Why didn't he stay with them?

It was probably Thomas in whom the truth began to dawn. He was shattered by Jesus' exact knowledge of his skeptical outburst (*"unless I see the nail marks in his hands and put my finger where the nails were, and put my hand into his side, I will not believe it,"* John 20:25). How had Jesus known? He had not appeared for the whole week since Thomas had said it, so no one could have told tales. Yet he had not been present when he said it . . . or had he?

So that was it! He could disappear, yet remain where he was. Gradually, it must have dawned on the disciples that he didn't necessarily go anywhere when he "left" them. Perhaps they blushed with embarrassment as they recalled some of their discussions in his apparent absence.

In a word, he was teaching them that his presence with them was no longer dependent on their physical senses. Whether they saw him or not, he was with them.

Furthermore, wherever they went he would already be there. When the two from Emmaus arrived breathless in Jerusalem to share their news, Jesus had beaten them to it. The first message to the disciples had been: *"he is going ahead of you into Galilee"* (Mark 16:7). No matter where they went, they'd find him there.

By the end of six weeks they learned the lesson. They could really believe he would be with them always, even to the end of history (Matthew 28:20). But this promise was directly linked to a command. They were to go to all the nations and make more disciples of Jesus (Matthew 28:19), preaching the good news to all creation (Mark 16:15). They were to preach repentance and forgiveness to all nations (Luke 24:47). As the Father had sent him into the world, he was sending them (John 20:21). They would be his witnesses to the ends of the earth (Acts 1:8).

Clearly the disciples were not going to stay together. They were going to be scattered around the world, with a divine commission.

The fact is that an embodied spirit is tied to one location: it is never possible to be in two places at once. The risen Jesus never appeared simultaneously to two separate groups or individuals. He could be present, even invisibly, with his disciples when they were together in one place, but how could he promise to be with them when they were widely separated? Certainly not in his resurrection body, whether visible or not.

Yet Jesus had prepared them for this (see John chapters 14–16).

He was going to leave them, but not *"orphaned."* He would send *"another"* to take his place (the Greek word means *"just like"*). He would be their *"Standby,"* just as Jesus had been. That is a better translation than "Comforter," which is too soft in English; the Greek *Paracletos* means someone *"called beside."* His name is *"the Holy Spirit."* He would be everything Jesus had been to them and more. He had been in Jesus, giving both the messages and miracles of his ministry – so he was not a complete stranger to the disciples. He had, in a sense, been *with* them, but would now be *in* them (John 14:7). This Holy Spirit is not just another person exactly like Jesus. He is the third person in the Trinity, for God is three persons in one. He is therefore so closely related to Jesus that he could be called *"the Spirit of Jesus"* or *"the Spirit of Christ"* (Acts 16:7; Romans 8:9). He has been described as Jesus' other self, his "alter ego."

Since the Father, Son and Spirit share the same nature and character, to experience the presence of any of them is to know the presence of all of them. To have the Spirit would be for the disciples as good as having Jesus with them – and even better, for he would be inside, not outside; and everywhere, not somewhere. Indeed, it meant having the Father and the Son indwelling them as well (John 14:23).

At some point there had to be a definite transfer from Jesus in his resurrection body *outside* them to the Spirit of Jesus *inside* them.

That is why the appearances did not end with a final disappearance, but with a visible departure, what we call his "ascension." They saw him go this time, until the clouds hid him from their eyes. An angel appeared and assured them he would one day return in bodily form.

But this was no sad farewell; no tears were shed at this separation. They had something to look forward to now, in the immediate as well as the ultimate future. Jesus would come back some day, but would send his Spirit *"in a few days"* (Acts 1:5). No wonder they returned from the eastern slopes of the Mount of Olives to the city of Jerusalem *"with great joy"* (Luke 24:52). The next few days were spent in praise and prayer in the temple itself.

On the next "first day of the week," at nine o'clock in the morning, as they gathered for the prayers in Solomon's Porch (where the mosque El-aqsa now stands), the Holy Spirit was poured on and into them, with audible wind and visible flames, right where they sat. Their praise exploded, but to their surprise they were using many new languages.

A crowd of thousands soon gathered around them, attracted by the noise. Peter and the eleven others stood up, while the rest remained seated and continued their worship. He seized the opportunity to preach his first-ever sermon, to which three thousand responded.

The rest is history. This event marked the beginning of an international mission that was to touch every part of the world, every nation, tribe, people and language (Revelation 7:9).

The disciples' boldness, risking their lives to announce that Jesus had risen in the very place where he had been executed as a criminal, deeply impressed the religious authorities who arrested them, especially as they were simple, uneducated people. It was put down to the fact that they had been under Jesus' influence in the past.

Wrong! It was because he was still with them and would be always and everywhere. They were not doing what they did *for* Jesus, but *with* him and in his name.

"Then the disciples went out and preached everywhere, and the Lord worked with them and confirmed his word by the signs that accompanied it" (Mark 16:20). The Gospel accounts only cover what Jesus *"began to do and to teach"* (Acts 1:1). His ministry on earth has continued to this day – and will do, until his bodily return.

7

The logical inference

When Peter preached that first sermon in Jerusalem on the day of Pentecost, it revolved around the central theme of the resurrection: *"Therefore let all Israel be assured of this: God has made this Jesus, whom you crucified, both Lord and Christ"* (Acts 2:36).

To understand how Peter came to make such an amazing claim, we need to realize that the resurrection had not only completely reversed the disciples' emotions; their thoughts had been radically changed as well. They now understood so clearly the meaning of the death and resurrection of Jesus, which had bewildered them at the time.

Imagine their state of mind while the body lay in the tomb. They had left everything to follow him, given him three of their best years, trusted him totally and found him utterly trustworthy. All their hopes for the future were pinned on him – but he had led them to disaster in such a short time. He seemed to know exactly what he was doing, but it had all gone terribly wrong. Perhaps that is why one of them had tried to get out of the situation with some capital to start another life.

It wasn't just a body that was buried in that tomb. It was the grave of their faith, not just in Jesus, but in God himself (how could a good God stand by and let it happen?). Their spirits were broken; their minds were confused; even their bodies were exhausted by it all (Luke 22:45). They must have felt they had nothing left to live for.

When Jesus rose, their whole outlook did a somersault. From being all wrong, everything became all right. Tragedy turned to triumph, gloom to glory.

Without the resurrection, Jesus himself would be an enigma

and his death on the cross a catastrophe. Now both his person and his work were seen in an entirely new light, the light of an empty tomb with the morning sun pouring through the reopened doorway.

The resurrection convinced the disciples that Jesus was who he claimed to be and that he had done what he came to do.

His person authenticated

Who was he? Everyone knew him as "Jesus of Nazareth," to distinguish him from many others who bore that name and because it was assumed he was born as well as brought up there. He had been the local carpenter for eighteen years.

When he began his public ministry, people had to revise their opinion. Three things left a profound impression on them.

First, what he *did*. His miracles with people – healing diseases, casting out demons, even raising the dead – were astonishing enough. His miracles with things – changing water into wine, multiplying food, controlling the weather – were even more amazing.

Second, what he *was*. Teaching stricter moral standards than anyone else had dared to demand, he lived up to them himself. Neither friend nor enemy could find a single fault in his character or conduct (John 8:46). His presence alone made others feel sinful (Luke 5:8). Yet sinners loved him and flocked to him.

Third, what he *said*. He claimed to have a unique relationship with God, daring to address him with the familiar *"Abba"* ("Dad" in English). He claimed to be able to forgive all sins and to be the one who would decide the destiny of every human being on Judgment Day. He said he had *"come,"* not been "born"; and therefore he had voluntarily chosen to become human. On one occasion he said he was already around when Abraham was born, two thousand years previously (they tried to stone him to death for that; John 8:56–59). He repeatedly began statements about himself with *"I am,"* which sounded suspiciously like the Hebrew name for God (*Yahweh*, a participle of the verb "to be").

Speculation about him was rife. Many called him a prophet; some saw him as *the* prophet promised by Moses (Deuteronomy 18:15–19; John 6:14). Others wondered if he could be the long-awaited Messiah or Christ. Among the more bizarre opinions was the notion of reincarnation, that he was one of the prophets returned in a different guise (Mark 8:28).

In the end, there are only three possible explanations for anyone making such claims for himself. He was mad, bad or God! A liar, lunatic or the Lord!

His traveling companions couldn't possibly think he was crazy, though at one stage his own family thought so and came to take him home (Mark 3:21). Nor could they see him as a deliberate deceiver. They were driven to the only alternative: he was the Christ, the Son of God. Peter was the first man to say this, Martha the first woman (Matthew 16:16; John 11:27).

But this was blasphemy in the eyes of the Jewish religious authorities. Jesus was arrested and accused of this crime, which carried the death sentence. When the court failed to find the required *"two or three witnesses"* to agree on his exact words, the case should have been dropped. The judge forced the prisoner to condemn himself by swearing him to answer the direct question whether he was the Christ, the Son of the Blessed One, to which Jesus replied: *"I am"* (Mark 14:61–62).

So Jesus was crucified for his pretensions to deity. To add to his suffering, he was mocked: *"Let him come down now from the cross, and we will believe in him. He trusts in God. Let God rescue him now if he wants him, for he said: 'I am the Son of God'"* (Matthew 27:42–43).

And God did nothing! He stayed away while the execution proceeded. Even Jesus, in his real humanity and the pressure of his pain, could not understand why (Matthew 27:46).

There was only one conclusion to be drawn – he was not God's Son after all. Surely God should have stopped the trial or at least prevented the sentence being carried out. But he didn't. It looked as if the verdict of the court was just, the defendant guilty and the punishment deserved.

The disciples were shattered, but the resurrection changed all that. In raising Jesus, God was declaring him innocent of blasphemy, reversing the verdict of the human court, canceling the sentence of death, preventing the inevitable process of corruption from touching the body of his Holy One (Psalm 16:10; Romans 1:4).

That is why they *"worshiped"* the risen Jesus, called him *"Lord"* and even *"God."* He was everything he had claimed to be. He had told the truth about himself – because he was the truth and the life.

It was all so blindingly clear now. But why had God let his Son die, especially in such a horrible way? Why allow him to go through such agony and anguish before rescuing him?

The risen Jesus himself gave them the answer. He had known all along what would happen. Indeed, he had told them on numerous occasions that he would be crucified, buried and raised. It was what he had come to do.

His work accepted

Between the resurrection and the ascension, Jesus did something with his disciples he had never done before. He gave them Bible studies. Of course, the only scriptures he knew were what we call the "Old Testament," but were then referred to as "the Law, the Prophets, and the Writings" – the five books of Moses called the Pentateuch, the historical and prophetic books covering the divine deeds and words in Israel's national life, the Psalms and the "Wisdom" literature.

Jesus took them through the whole of these, pointing out everything relevant to himself. He must have known the scriptures well and by context (there were no chapter and verse numbers then).

The first time he did this was on the road to Emmaus (Luke 24:27), but he did the same later in Jerusalem (Luke 24:44–45). His purpose was to show them that his death had been planned a very long time ago. It was all in God's purpose; it was not an accident.

It had been indirectly foreshadowed in ancient events. Abraham's sacrifice of Isaac in his early thirties on Mount Moriah, later Golgotha or Calvary, replaced by a ram with its head caught in thorns, was a "type" in Genesis. The Passover lamb, killed at 3pm on the day before Passover, was the type in Exodus. The scapegoat in Leviticus, the brass serpent in Numbers, the curse on anyone whose body was hung on a tree in Deuteronomy, the whole sacrificial system of the Temple – these and many more must have figured in his exposition.

It had been directly predicted by the prophets. David was a prophet as well as a king (2 Samuel 23:2; Acts 2:30). Psalm 22 not only gave Jesus the words to express his anguish on the cross (verse 1 reads: *"My God, my God, why have you forsaken me?"*); it describes the piercing of his hands and feet, the gambling for his clothes and the mockery of the spectators – a situation which David himself never experienced.

But it was surely the great prophetic message of Isaiah that Jesus opened up more than any other scripture. In the first half of the book the prophet looked forward to the coming king, who would bring peace and justice. In the second half another figure appeared, a *"servant"* who would suffer and die for the sins of his people. Neither Isaiah himself nor any of his people realized these two portraits were of the same person (most Jews still don't). So they could not understand that he would have to be the suffering servant *before* he could be the reigning king, much less anticipate that these two functions would be widely separated in time, involving *two* comings of the Messiah.

One passage (Isaiah 52:13–53:12) is treasured as one of the clearest and most moving explanations of why the cross was necessary. *"But he was pierced for our transgressions, he was crushed for our iniquities; the punishment that brought us peace was upon him, and by his wounds we are healed"* (Isaiah 53:5).

The innocent was a substitute for the guilty. Jesus had told the disciples he had come to *"give his life as a ransom for many"* (Mark 10:45). During the last three hours on the cross he went through "hell" for us – darkness, thirst, agony and above all, separation from God. His obedience unto death, even death on the cross (Philippians 2:8), was a victory over all the forces of evil (Colossians 2:15; John 12:31).

Isaiah had also predicted that when the Messiah had given his life as an offering for the sins of the people, God would raise him to the highest position (Isaiah 53:10–12).

This means that the resurrection not only proves that Jesus was who he had claimed to be, but also that he had accomplished what he had come to do. It was God's way of saying that his sacrifice was accepted, his atonement complete. So Jesus cried out *"it is finished,"* just before he died.

8

The fundamental significance

There is much, much more to the resurrection than we have already shared. So what is its fundamental significance?

The first thing to realize is that it was an act of God himself. The New Testament writers usually say that Jesus was *"raised,"* rather than that he "rose." He had raised others, but God raised him.

The next thing to understand is that though redemption was the object, God's intervention was an act of creation. It was the first such since he finished making the whole universe! That is what made it so significant.

It was not just the beginning of a new relationship. It was the dawn of a new age. It was the start of a new creation. It was the *"first fruits"* of a whole new world.

There are two obvious clues in the record of the resurrection. One is the nature of his risen body. The other is the day on which he rose.

The new body

That he had a real body after he rose from the dead, we have already established. It was a material body that could be touched and could interact with our real world.

Yet equally, it was a very remarkable body, free from natural limitations and perfectly subject to the spirit using it. It could be visible or invisible, apparently according to the will of its owner. It could likewise be tangible or intangible, passing through locked doors (John 20:26); the stone was therefore not rolled away to let him out, but to let others in. That body could move rapidly and effortlessly from one place to another. And finally, it floated up into the atmosphere, and on through the stratosphere for all we know.

Jesus had done none of these things before he died. The nearest action would be walking on water, but Peter did the same.

Quite simply, the body was very different. It belonged to the same person and it looked very similar in dimension, features and even disfigurements. Yet had it been the identical one, it would have aged and died again. It was a supernatural body, just as at home in heaven as on earth, perhaps more so.

How did it come about? God could have used the old body as resource material, or even melted it down to the energy from which matter is formed, so that it could pass through the cloth (leaving a scorched image of the body, as some claim for the shroud of Turin) and the sealed stone, to be re-formed on the outside. On the other hand, he could cause the old body to "pass away," to dissolve into nothing and create a completely new body from scratch.

One thing is certain. Jesus had entered into a new mode of existence, beyond the reach of age, death and decay, and also beyond the reach of the cause of this humiliating process – moral evil. He had *"died to sin"* (Romans 6:10).

There is one other pointer to the resurrection as an act of creation – the day of the week on which it happened.

The eighth day

If we are not sure about the day on which he died, we are quite sure about the day on which he was raised. The witnesses are unanimous. It was the *"first day of the week."*

Humanly speaking, it was a strange day for God to choose. It was not his special day, the Sabbath, that day devoted wholly to him, when work gave way to worship. Nor was it that special Sabbath that ended the Passover; that was probably the following Wednesday if the seven-day feast began the previous Thursday.

It was a normal working day, when everybody would have returned to their daily job. Of course, the disciples were still in a state of mourning and, in any case, had not been to ordinary work for three years. And they, together with thousands of others from Galilee, were visiting Jerusalem for the feast.

Divinely speaking, it was the only day that was right for God. It was his first working day as well! It was the very day when he began his work of creation, the day on which he commanded light to overcome the original darkness – which constituted the *"evening and morning"* of the first day. This, incidentally, explains why Jews count each new day from 6pm and why Jesus could have been raised anytime after 6pm on what we call Saturday.

Giving Jesus a new body was God's first act of creation since he finished work on our present universe (Genesis 2:2). Since then he had done many other things, including the maintenance of what he had made. But he had not done any more creating. His *"seventh day"* of rest lasted through all the centuries covered by our Old Testament.

The word "new" hardly ever occurs in the Old Testament. The only text that springs readily to mind is: *"there is nothing new under the sun"* (Ecclesiastes 1:9). Yet the New Testament is full of the word. What caused the change?

God has gone back to work! He has made a start on his new creation. He is ultimately *"making everything new"* (Revelation 21:5). The second week of creation has begun. We are living in the eighth day of creation.

The very first part of the old creation to be made new was the body of Jesus, his Son. As his old body disappeared, so the whole heaven and earth will one day have *"passed away"* (Revelation 21:1). Jesus is the *"firstborn over all creation"* and the *"firstborn from among the dead"* (Colossians 1:15, 18). So Jesus' resurrection was only the beginning of a work of God that will change the entire universe.

One surprising practical effect on the disciples was that they changed their regular day of worship, from Saturday to Sunday! For Jews to do this is incredible. Together with circumcision, Sabbath observance was a fundamental pillar of their distinctive culture. It was one of the ten commandments given by God through angels to Moses. Centuries of tradition reinforced the habit.

They were not consciously trying to be different, to distinguish their faith from that of their fathers. Nor was Sunday a new Sabbath, a day of rest (it would not be that for any Christians for another 300 years – until the Roman Emperor Constantine was "converted" and imposed it by law).

The disciples were simply reflecting God himself, bringing their worship up to date with his contemporary activity. It was no longer appropriate to commemorate his day of rest, for that was over. They were celebrating the fact that he was back at work. One early tradition refers to Sunday as "the eighth day."

The new creation had burst in upon the old. The new age had dawned. The future had become present.

Even their old songs of praise took on new meaning:

The stone the builders rejected
has become the capstone;
the Lord *has done this,*
and it is marvelous in our eyes.
This is the day the Lord *has made;*
let us rejoice and be glad in it.

(Psalm 118:22–24)

9

The universal consequence

If the resurrection of Jesus was the inauguration of the new creation, there are far-reaching consequences for everyone and everything else.

Both our human race and our physical environment are to die and rise again. The resurrection means that this is possible and even certain.

It is both the ground and guarantee of our future. We can confidently expect that one day there will be a re-created world populated by re-created human beings. God is to be praised because *"in his great mercy he has given us new birth into a living hope through the resurrection of Jesus Christ from the dead, and into an inheritance that can never perish, spoil or fade"* (1 Peter 1:3–4).

Resurrection of the dead

Human existence passes through three phases: embodied spirit, disembodied spirit, re-embodied spirit.

We have already seen that Jesus went through all three in less than a week. For us it takes rather longer! Nobody but Jesus has entered the third. We pass from the first to the second as individuals, on different dates. But we shall pass from the second to the third all together, on the same date – or rather, as we shall see, on just two dates.

For there are just two kinds of people in the world: righteous and wicked, believers and unbelievers, saints and sinners. There are two destinies awaiting the human race.

First comes the *"resurrection of the righteous"* (Luke 14:14). Elsewhere this is described as the resurrection *"from the dead"* (Luke 20:35; Acts 4:2; Philippians 3:11), the same phrase that is used of Jesus (1 Peter 1:3). It is also referred to as the *"first"* resurrection, because *"the rest of the dead"* are not raised until much later (Revelation 20:5).

This takes place on the day that Jesus himself returns to planet earth in his resurrection body (see 1 Thessalonians 4:13–18). The believers who have already died will be the first to get their new bodies. Those still alive will not die at all but their bodies will be changed instantaneously, in the blink of an eye (1 Corinthians 15:52).

As we saw in chapter 2, Greek thinking had great difficulty with the idea of re-embodiment. It is not surprising that church members in Corinth were reluctant to believe it. But for their skepticism we might never have had the most illuminating passage on the subject in the whole New Testament: 1 Corinthians 15.

Apparently the Corinthians simply could not imagine how anyone could get another body. Nicodemus had similar problems with the idea of being *"born again."* Both he and they were making the same mistake in thinking that the second birth and the second body would be exactly the same as the first.

Paul tried to explain by taking analogies from nature. When a seed is buried in the ground it disintegrates and dies, yet somehow from it there comes a new seed, similar and yet not the same. There are many different kinds of bodies on earth: humans, birds, animals, fish; the same applies to the heavens: sun, moon, and stars. In other words, the Creator can create any kind of body he likes.

Our new bodies will be quite different from the old ones, in many ways a complete contrast. The old one was perishable, lowly and weak; the new one will be imperishable, glorious and powerful. This is because the old was natural, while the new will be spiritual.

But this does not mean we shall be intangible and unreal. The adjective describes our supernatural origin rather than nature. Our old body came to us from earth, quite literally, through the first Adam – which is why it finishes up where it began. Our new body will come to us from heaven, through Jesus, the *"last Adam."*

The likeness of the progenitor is passed on to all descendants. As we have borne the likeness of Adam, so our new bodies will be just like Jesus' *"glorious"* resurrection body (Philippians 3:21). While we struggle with physical limitations and handicaps, we groan with impatience, waiting eagerly for what Paul describes as our coming of age, *"the redemption of our bodies"* (Romans 8:23).

It is in this context that Paul declares that the whole creation shares our frustration! Our present universe is also under the bondage of decay. It also has a sentence of death on it (scientists call it "the second law of thermodynamics" – the fixed amount of energy is becoming less and less usable).

The resurrection of our bodies will be the precursor of a recreated universe, a new heaven and a new earth. New bodies need a new place in which to live.

Recreation of the universe

This world is now too polluted both physically and morally, to recover. It is going to die.

The death will be violent, a bang rather than a whimper, a sudden catastrophe rather than a gradual decline.

The earth will be destroyed by fire, as it was once by a flood. Even the elements in outer space will be incinerated (2 Peter 3:10). So this is much, much more than a humanly created nuclear holocaust. It is more like the reduction of every atom in the universe to its primal energy. The God who packed every atom can split every atom.

This catastrophic conclusion to history is frequently mentioned in the New Testament (Matthew 24:35; Hebrews 1:10–12, quoting Psalm 102:25–27; Revelation 21:1; etc.). Heaven and earth are to *"pass away."* The physical universe will come to an end. The God who created it will destroy it.

Yet out of the ashes will arise a new heaven and a new earth. God has determined that all things are to be made new (Revelation 21:1, 5).

This amazing prospect had first been revealed to a Hebrew prophet (Isaiah 65:17–18). But it was the resurrection of Jesus that guaranteed it, his body being the very first part of the old creation to be dissolved and re-created. The rest of the renovation would inevitably follow.

Such a hope is bound to affect the Christian attitude to this planet. The responsibility to be good stewards of the earth entrusted to us, husbanding its resources and protecting it from abuse and exploitation, is very clear in the Bible. Adam was to look after the garden of Eden. The law of Moses forbade the wanton destruction of trees in war and insisted on the land having regular fallow rest and recuperation. So Christians are concerned, or should be, about ecology and the environment.

But the knowledge that this is not the only earth we shall ever have to live on prevents the despair or panic that can motivate the "green" movement. This can be pursued with a religious fervor that is in danger of replacing Father God with "mother earth," bordering on a revival of the fertility cults which were such a snare for ancient Israel. It is idolatry to become devoted to the creation rather than the Creator; it is to exchange the truth for a lie (Romans 1:25).

The truth is that our future and the earth's are in God's hands. And he has already told us what he is going to do with both. Both will come to an end – and a new beginning. The God who raised Jesus from the dead will do it.

But what happens to the human individual between death and resurrection? For Christians their disembodied spirits will be fully conscious of being with Jesus himself and being *"away from the body"* will mean that no earthly distractions will interfere with the joy of being *"at home with the Lord"* (2 Corinthians 5:8). Though Paul did not relish being without a body and longed for his new one as soon as possible (2 Corinthians 5:4), he said that to be on the earth is to be *"away from the Lord"* who is in heaven (2 Corinthians 5:6). Therefore he desired *"to depart and be with Christ, which is better by far"* (Philippians 1:23).

As for the others, they have nothing to look forward to after death. Yet they do not cease to be. Their disembodied spirits continue to exist.

We have so far only considered the future from the Christian angle, considering the first resurrection, that *"of the righteous,"* for *"those who belong to"* Christ, *"when he comes"* (1 Corinthians 15:23).

But there is another resurrection later, for *"the rest of the dead"* (Revelation 20:5), regardless of social status, *"great and small"* (Revelation 20:12). Daniel, Jesus and Paul all stated their belief that the wicked would be raised with new bodies, no less than the righteous (Daniel 12:2; John 5:29; Acts 24:15), though, as we have seen, this will be on a different date.

And for a different destiny. For this second resurrection, which includes even those lost at sea and never buried (Revelation 20:13), will immediately be followed by the final judgment of the human race. God has delegated the awesome task of deciding the fate of every human being who has ever lived to his Son, the Lord Jesus Christ (Matthew 25:31–32; Acts 17:31; Romans 2:16).

While everyone will receive a resurrected body, not everyone will enter the re-created universe. That is the solemn truth disclosed in the last few pages of the Bible.

The reason is simple. God will not allow his creation to be ruined a second time. Since moral pollution is the source of all other kind of corruption, the new world will be the *"home of righteousness"* (2 Peter 3:13). That is why *"nothing impure will ever enter it, nor will anyone who does what is shameful or deceitful"* (Revelation 21:27). The New Testament lists over one hundred and twenty "sins" that would disqualify us – from sexual offences through the obvious crimes like murder or theft, to religious perversions of an occult kind, and on to such things as pride, greed and envy, even including cowardice and unbelief.

What is the destiny of those who refuse to disassociate themselves from such attitudes and actions? There is a place *"prepared"* for them – hell. Variously described as *"the lake of fire"* or *"the second death"* (Revelation 21:8), its essence is the torment of being shut out of God's creation forever.

That's the bad news. But there is good news, too. No one need suffer this dreadful fate. Any human being can live in that new universe, on one condition – that they are willing to be prepared for it now, willing to receive forgiveness (made possible by the death of Jesus) and holiness (made possible by his resurrection).

The process of re-creation can and must begin for the individual person while still in the old body and the old world. In this life, here and now. How?

10

The practical experience

There is one great difference between the two weeks of creation. In the first God began by making the heaven and the earth; he ended by making men and women. This time he is making new men and women at the beginning and will make the new heaven and earth at the end.

The order is reversed because of his love for us! He could have wiped everything out and started again from scratch. But he loves us too much to do that and wants to give as many of us as possible the opportunity to be part of his new creation, even though we have rebelled against his love, provoked his anger – and killed his Son!

That he should still be willing to have us, even want us, is quite incredible. Yet he has done everything to make it possible for us to share in this wonderful future he has planned. All that is what we mean by the word *"grace."* It is undeserved mercy for sinners.

But it does involve a radical change in us. If we entered the new universe as we are, we'd ruin that one as quickly as we've ruined this one! Even before we get a new body, we need a new spirit within us. David's prayer, after his adultery with Bathsheba and murder of her husband, speaks for us all: *"Create in me a pure heart, O God, and renew a steadfast spirit within me"* (Psalm 51:10).

The good news is that God, the maker of heaven and earth, is able and willing to do just that for us, using the same power with which he raised Jesus from the dead.

He is already doing it. Millions have found that they have received new life – through faith in the risen Christ. *"If anyone is in Christ, there is a new creation; the old has gone, the new has come!"* (2 Corinthians 5:17). Significantly this happens more often on a Sunday, the *"first day of the week,"* than any other day.

This salvaging process begins when someone hears the gospel about the death, burial and resurrection of Jesus and responds to it. Jesus' risen appearances were inseparably linked with his command to tell the whole world about him. All the records emphasize this mandate (Matthew 28:19; Mark 16:15; Luke 24:47; John 20:21; Acts 1:8). The mission of the disciples was to be universal yet individual – to go into the entire world, preach the gospel to every creature and make disciples of all nations.

The objective was to prepare people for the new world, even while they were still in this one. For the *"age to come"* had already broken into the *"present evil age"* (both terms were familiar to Jews). The kingdom of God was *"at hand,"* within reach; it could be *"entered"* now, though it could not be *"inherited"* in full until later.

But the gospel requires a sincere and voluntary response. The objective fact of the resurrection only becomes a subjective experience when the grace of God is personally appropriated. The process of re-creation begins and continues in the cooperation between divine and human action. God brings about an inward spiritual renewal but expects this to be translated into outward moral reform. Together, these constitute the process of resurrection that will be consummated when a new body completes the new person.

Inward spiritual renewal

The right response to the gospel is a determination to be finished with sin, known as *"repentance"* (Luke 3:8; Acts 26:20) and a personal commitment to trust and obey the risen Jesus forever, which is *"faith"* (Romans 10:8–10).

This begins with two baptisms, one in water, the other in the Holy Spirit (John 3:5; Titus 3:5). Both are directly connected with the resurrection of Jesus.

Baptism in water transfers the facts of the gospel into our own lives. We are baptized into the death of Jesus, buried with him in water and raised with him to live a new life (Romans 6:1–4). It is not the washing of the body but the cleansing of the conscience which makes this clean start possible; in this way baptism *"saves you by the resurrection of Jesus Christ"* (1 Peter 3:21). Our sins have been forgiven and *"washed away"* (Acts 2:38; 22:16).

But cleaning up the past will not keep us clean in the future. To live the new life will require a strength we do not have. That, too, will be taken care of.

Baptism in the Holy Spirit fills us with the same power with which God raised his Son from the tomb (Romans 1:4). Even these mortal bodies will be revitalized by this divine influx (Romans 8:11).

Since he is the *Holy* Spirit, holiness is now a possible attainment, not an impossible dream. It is not just that we can live *like* Christ; we can live *with* him and *in* him. His risen life is ours (Galatians 2:20).

He does all this for us when we put ourselves in his hands. But if this is to be continually effective and eventually completed, there is another aspect to experiencing the resurrection.

Outward moral reform

Holiness requires human effort (Hebrews 12:14). New Testament verbs are a balanced mixture of the indicative and imperative. The former describe the divine contribution to our salvation; the latter the human cooperation.

The paradox of new life in Christ is expressed in the maxim: "become what you are." We are called *"saints,"* so must live up to our calling. We have been sanctified, so must seek sanctification; we have been crucified, buried and raised with Christ, so must now apply that to our daily lives.

"Since, then, you have been raised with Christ, set your hearts on things above, where Christ is seated at the right hand of God" (Colossians 3:1). The risen life is already ours in principle, but needs to be put into practice.

We must *"put off,"* even *"put to death,"* the old life. The flesh, the old nature, must be crucified and buried. The mind and heart need to be consciously and deliberately severed from the old motives like lust, greed, pride, envy, anger and hatred.

However, though these matters are settled in the mind and heart, they are expressed in the body (Matthew 5:28). It is precisely because he is going to raise us as he raised Jesus that our bodies cannot be given to promiscuity or joined to a prostitute (1 Corinthians 6:13–18).

We have been given the grace to say *"No"* (Titus 2:11–12). But a life that is only made up of negatives, of things not done, will be empty, miserable and dangerous (Matthew 12:44). We must also *"put on,"* or *"clothe"* ourselves, with the new life, the risen life of Christ. New virtues need to be deliberately and consciously embraced – compassion, kindness, humility, gentleness, patience, forgiveness and above all, love.

Not ours, but his. It is no use trying to act like Jesus. We never could. It's a case of choosing to let the risen Jesus live his life out in us. *"I have been crucified with Christ and I no longer live, but Christ lives in me. The life I live in the body, I live by faith in the Son of God"* (Galatians 2:20).

Thus does the historical event become our present experience. The transformation of our daily lives is a demonstration of his risen life.

11

The crucial importance

Although the cross has become the universal symbol of the Christian, it speaks of death, especially in the form of a crucifix. An empty tomb would be more appropriate, though it is more difficult to depict and would perhaps still be associated with the dead.

The apostles preached *"Christ crucified"* (1 Corinthians 1:23), but a more appropriate translation would be *"Christ having been crucified."* He should no more be thought of as still on the cross (even on Good Friday) than as still in a manger (as so many do at Christmas). Unlike all the great figures of history who were alive and are now dead, Jesus can say *"I was dead, and behold I am alive forever and ever"* (Revelation 1:18).

The resurrection was at the heart of the gospel for those first apostles (see Acts 2:22–36; 3:15, 26; 4:10, 33; 5:30; 10:40–41; 13:29–39; 17:31). It is no exaggeration to say that for them everything else hung on this one fact. Without it, they had no gospel. It was as crucial as that.

There is a widespread notion today that belief in a bodily resurrection of Jesus is not essential to the Christian faith and life. It is said that if his bones were discovered to be still lying buried somewhere in the Middle East, this need make little or no difference to his followers. Even bishops within the Church are saying such things, probably trying to remove what is an offence to contemporary thinking.

It is said that we could still admire and revere Jesus, seek to follow his moral and spiritual teaching and emulate his willingness to die for his principles. Many have sought to do this, from Tolstoy to Gandhi. Why insist on believing such an extraordinary story? Surely many more would "follow"

Jesus if they were not expected to accept such an intellectual impossibility!

The apostles would have been astonished at such a line of thought. They had had three days to find out what it meant to follow a Jesus who has not risen. It led to disaster and despair, and even total loss of faith for Judas.

For them, and for us, what is at stake is the truth. Jesus himself hated all lies, and called them the devil's native language (John 8:44). All forms of deception, especially hypocrisy, were anathema to him. He claimed always to speak the truth, even to be the truth (John 14:6).

Yet if he was not raised from the dead, then the religion he founded is based on a lie.

Based on a lie

Christianity would be the biggest fraud in history. Some fifteen hundred million people have been fooled. Propagators of the faith are no better than confidence tricksters.

Who should we hold responsible for this gigantic hoax? Presumably those who originally foisted it on a gullible public – the apostles who invented the story and the New Testament writers who perpetuated it.

Did Jesus himself not plant the first seeds of the idea by predicting it himself on more than one occasion? Had he not done so, it would never have entered their imagination.

This would not be the only case in which Jesus himself would have been lying. All that he said about himself, his claims to be the unique Son of God, to be able to forgive sins, to be the final judge of every human being – all these assertions would be false, since God himself apparently disowned him, allowing him to die the death he deserved.

How could we trust such a person to be right in anything else he said, when he could be so deluded about himself? It is not just that we'd find it hard to believe in him; it would also be difficult to believe in the God he believed in. How could we ever believe that God really was a loving Father, if the person who told us that was so untrustworthy?

We'd lose more than faith if Jesus did not rise from the dead. We'd lose forgiveness. How can we ever have our sins cancelled unless they have been atoned for, the penalty paid and justice satisfied? Christians have assumed that this is what happened on the cross – *"Christ died for our sins"* (1 Corinthians 15:3). But how can we know that his suffering and sacrifice released us from our debt to divine justice? If Jesus was not raised, we are *"still in our sins"* (1 Corinthians 15:17), and our faith is futile.

Even worse, our hopes for the future are dashed. We will never have the fullness of life with a body that can express us and relate to the environment. The earth itself will die a lingering death, with dwindling food and fuel resources, and accelerated pollution of air and water. Oblivion is not an option. Truly, *"if only for this life we have hope in Christ, we are to be pitied more than all people"* (1 Corinthians 15:19). Christians would lose more by death than anyone else!

Christian faith could be considered dangerous and cruel in raising false hopes. If Christ has not been raised, then we have to say that all our beliefs are based on a lie. This fatal flaw affects everything else. The wise seeker after God would have to look elsewhere, probably concluding that each religion helps some and none helps all.

Bound by the truth

But if it is true that Jesus is alive today, we can no longer take refuge in relativism. We are confronted with absolutes, and we can only accept or refuse the truth. If we reject it, we deceive ourselves and lose touch with reality, for in both the Hebrew and Greek languages, "truth" and "reality" are one and the same word.

If the resurrection was real, then we have to face the reality that Jesus was really who he claimed to be – the only Son of the living God.

This means that God himself, the creator of our whole universe has entered our space-time world in the person of the Lord Jesus Christ. This is the most important thing we can ever know about God. He has met us on our own ground to establish a personal relationship with us.

This immediately sets Christianity apart from other religions. It is not a religion – it is a *revelation*! God has revealed the truth to us, not just in words, but in the Word made flesh (John 1:14). Above all, it is a *relationship* – with God the Father, through his Son, by his Spirit.

If this is the truth, then Jesus is *"the way, the truth and the life"* and no one can come to the Father except through him (John 14:6). If this is the truth, then *"salvation is found in no one else, for there is no other name under heaven given to people by which we must be saved"* (Acts 4:12). If this is the truth, there is only *"one God and one mediator between God and human beings, Christ Jesus, himself human, who gave himself as a ransom for all"* (1 Timothy 2:5).

All religions denying this are false. They may contain some elements of truth, but insofar as they ignore or deny the way that God has provided for human beings to know him, they lead people away from the truth. For the truth is a person, Jesus Christ.

The resurrection is the linchpin of the Christian faith and life. Without it, everything would fall apart.

12

The legal acceptance

If so much hangs on the resurrection, it is hardly surprising that it has been the focus of so much discussion and disagreement. The arguments about it are as heated today as they have ever been.

In fact, the apostles didn't argue the case for believing that Jesus was alive, they simply announced it, with the boldness of those who were absolutely sure. Even their critics were impressed with their confidence (Acts 4:13).

Everyone then knew their story could easily be checked – the apostles were proclaiming Jesus' resurrection within a short time of his burial and a short distance from his grave. But we are not. It all happened so long ago and far away. Two thousand years have passed, during which no one has produced either the dead or living body of Jesus. So how can we know the truth?

The scientific methods of observation, deduction and experimentation cannot be applied here, because like other historical events the resurrection was unique and cannot be repeated in a laboratory setting. The effects of an event can be attested, but not its cause or content.

However, both historians and the legal profession have developed their own criteria to establish the reality of happenings that they have not personally witnessed. Through this, they cannot offer absolute proof, but can reach a high degree of probability "beyond reasonable doubt."

Two kinds of evidence are considered: first-hand accounts, especially of eyewitnesses, and indirect circumstantial evidence that points in the same direction. For the resurrection, both are available.

Eyewitness accounts

The New Testament documents are the primary source of information. They can and should be treated in the same way as any other ancient records, when seeking to establish historical accuracy.

Yet this must be done with integrity. Alas, many people have come to them with skeptical assumptions and prejudices.

First, it is assumed that they were written so long after the event as to allow myth and legend to corrupt the memory. Actually, it is now believed that most of the New Testament writings, if not all, were completed before 80 AD, perhaps even before 64 AD. Certainly within a generation, the written accounts were circulating, and they embodied the spoken accounts already being propagated.

Second, it is assumed that the documents have been corrupted in transmission down the centuries. But we now have about 25,000 early manuscript copies (compared with about 650 of Homer's *Iliad*). This has enabled scholars to recover the original text and we have the New Testament "substantially as it was written" (one scholar estimates accuracy at 98%). This puts authenticity beyond doubt.

Third, it is assumed that the authors were biased and were imposing their later beliefs on the facts. Yet the New Testament writers claim to have gone out of their way to stick to the facts (Luke 1:1–3; Acts 1:1–3), to avoid *"cleverly invented stories"* and to base everything on the testimony of eyewitnesses (2 Peter 1:16). If the facts led to their faith, why should they be accused of letting their faith distort the facts?

When their testimony is examined impartially, the authenticity is impressive. As has been already mentioned (in chapter 4), even apparent discrepancies underline rather than undermine the independence and integrity of the witnesses.

The historical basis for the life, death and resurrection of Jesus may be said to be more soundly established than for any other prominent figure of his time. Skeptics may be surprised by the amount of supportive data.

A significant number of leading figures in the legal profession have been convinced of the testimony of the gospels, including many prominent judges. One lawyer, Frank Morrison, set out to write a book disproving the resurrection and found himself persuaded by the evidence to do just the opposite in his book, *Who Moved the Stone?* (IVP, 1982).

Circumstantial evidence

Circumstantial evidence plays an important part in establishing facts, and if particularly strong can stand on its own. Known facts that confirm the testimony have a cumulative effect if they all seem to point in the same direction. They are particularly impressive when there is no other adequate explanation for them.

There are five such circumstances that are difficult to explain, unless Jesus rose from the dead.

First, the missing body. No bones have been found, no grave discovered and revered as a shrine. Could it have been hidden without a trace or any leaked information? Hostile authorities must have had a vested interest in finding it, but never did.

Second, Sunday worship. As already mentioned, it is almost incredible for Jews, of all people, to forsake the revered and ancient tradition of their people, to worship on the first working day of the week. It would have been socially inconvenient and extremely unpopular, to say the least. Something extraordinary must have happened to create this "Lord's Day" (Revelation 1:10), which has persisted until now and has spread to many parts of the world.

Third, the changed disciples. The contrast is clear. Just before Jesus' death they were panicking deserters, fearful for their lives. Immediately after it, they were broken men, cowering behind locked doors. Yet a short time later, they were publicly accusing the authorities of Jesus' murder and announcing his resurrection from the dead. It is stretching credulity to the limit to suggest that though they had been unwilling to die with their friend, they would now be willing to do so for a fraud!

Fourth, the existence of the Church. Within two months, thousands believed the apostles' claim that Jesus had risen. Now there are millions, over one-third of the world's population, for whom Easter Sunday is the most important day of the year. The growth and spread of the Christian Church is a historical phenomenon that requires explanation.

Fifth, changed lives. The Church is made up of individuals who testify that believing in a living Lord Jesus has brought healing to diseased bodies, forgiveness to guilty consciences, peace to troubled minds, love to hardened hearts, hope to flagging spirits, strength to weak wills and many other personal benefits. They can also point to numerous social and political byproducts of this personal change. Such testimonies cannot be lightly cast aside.

None of these five facts may seem conclusive by itself, but all of them taken together make a convincing case for the resurrection. The onus is on those who are not persuaded to find an alternative yet adequate explanation.

Lawyers have frequently observed that eyewitness accounts plus circumstantial evidence are enough to convince any jury "beyond reasonable doubt" and enable them to reach a unanimous verdict.

If faith demanded more, it would hardly be faith at all.

13

The general reluctance

While millions do believe in the resurrection, millions more do not. Many have never heard about it, but many others have – and still do not believe it.

Those who seek to spread the good news that death has met its match, encounter a general reluctance to accept it. Many people seem positively hostile, determined to find another interpretation of the basic facts behind the resurrection story.

There have been five main theories used to explain it away.

First, theft. Supposedly, the body was stolen by the disciples to "fake" the resurrection. This is the oldest hypothesis (Matthew 28:13). The guards were bribed to say the disciples had stolen it while they were sleeping on duty. Augustine asked how they knew it was the disciples if they were asleep! Also, if the disciples had successfully stolen and hidden the corpse, it is very odd that they would be happy to die themselves (as most of them did) for what they knew to be a lie.

Second, error. Those who buried Jesus went to the wrong tomb. This is surprising, as it was a private tomb and almost certainly the only one in the garden. Even more surprisingly, no one apparently realized it was the wrong one or went looking for the right one. Even the angels must have been in error!

Third, hallucination. The disciples were "seeing things." That this should happen to a tax collector like Mathew, a guerilla fighter like Simon, a fisherman like Peter or John, an unbelieving relative like James, or five hundred at once in broad daylight seems unlikely. That the hallucinations should be spread over six weeks and then abruptly cease makes the theory even less likely. The appearances were neither expected nor sought, particularly by the hardened Pharisee, Saul of Tarsus.

Fourth, swoon. Jesus was not really dead; he recovered in the cool of the tomb. Apparently suffering no ill-effects from having been flogged, nailed to a cross for six hours, having a spear thrust through his chest and being without food and water for three days, he pushed two tons of stone away and persuaded his disciples that he was alive and well. It doesn't say much for the efficiency of the execution squad and begs many questions. But it was a popular theory in the nineteenth century.

Fifth, plot. This is a twentieth-century variant on the same theme. Apparently, the whole thing was a conspiracy, master-minded by Jesus himself, to fake a fulfillment of Messianic prophecies. He arranged to be secretly drugged on the cross to feign death and had someone hidden in the tomb (one version says it was a doctor) to help with his "resurrection." These convenient props are, of course, sheer speculation.

Many other commentators have reviewed and refuted these bizarre surmises in great detail. Their handling of the evidence seems very arbitrary, as if the theorists feel free to pick and choose whatever they like and reject the rest. Some accept that the tomb was empty; others don't. Some think the disciples knew what they were doing; others don't. In fact, the hypotheses seem to cancel each other out!

Yet their highly selective use of the records suggests that a preconceived answer has shaped the questions. Presuppositions can blind people to the truth. But are the blinkers mental or moral in origin?

Mental reservation

There is a mental barrier. Modern philosophy has been profoundly influenced by Newtonian physics. Nature is still thought of as a closed system governed by its own inherent laws, in which every effect has a "natural" cause.

Such an outlook cannot conceive of supernatural intervention from outside in the form of a miracle. God may have created the universe but cannot now control it; it controls itself (a philosophy called "deism," formerly held by many scientists). It may even have created itself as well ("monism" draws no distinction between mind and matter, creator and creation; all is one unit of being).

The biblical philosophy is "theism," the belief that God created the universe, which is still under his control. He is free to do whatever he wants with it and in it, his will only subject to his character.

Since the resurrection is the most outstanding miracle in history, an instantaneous act of special creation, it runs counter to contemporary thinking. To many the question is not: "Did it happen?" but "Could it happen?" Naturalistic thinking says it *couldn't,* so obviously it *didn't.* Any apparent evidence must be squeezed into a "natural" explanation or discarded.

More recently, theologians within the Christian Church are reinterpreting the resurrection in purely "spiritual" terms. They do not dismiss the accounts; they "demythologize" them, telling us that they must be seen as descriptions of faith, not fact. The "appearances" were subjective, not objective, and it was the faith of the disciples, not the body of Jesus, which "rose again." It was Jesus' influence that lived on, rather than his person, in the disciples' memory and ministry. The resurrection was a psychological experience, not a physical event.

Advocates of this approach claim to be making it easier for the modern mind to accept the gospel by removing an unnecessary offence. Perhaps it is also to enable them to maintain their Christian profession while accepting a "secular" world view.

Whatever their motive, such a compromise, rather than defending the gospel, reduces it to little more than a sanctified humanism. It is precisely the supernatural and miraculous act of creation that makes the resurrection the harbinger of the new creation, the inauguration of the new age.

From one angle this new theology is quite old, recalling the ancient Greeks and their separation of body and soul, the physical and spiritual. Human beings have again put asunder what God has joined together.

The resurrection is thus removed from the real world and isolated in mysticism. The result is to lose sight of the coming new creation and to become totally absorbed in the fleeting life of this old world. The hope of Jesus' bodily return to earth in the second coming becomes an irrelevance, an anachronism.

This is too high a price to pay to make the gospel credible to contemporary society. And it may soon prove to be a major tactical blunder, in view of another modern trend.

While theologians have been accommodating their ideas to naturalistic concepts, scientists have been steadily moving away from the idea of nature as a closed and consistent system.

Quantum physics sees nature as more open, even chaotic, more flexible than fixed, more unpredictable than determined, more mobile than static.

This new attitude does not reestablish the idea of creation, much less belief in a Creator, but it is much more sympathetic to the possibility. Scientists are much less ready to say what *can* or cannot happen and are more ready to acknowledge the limits of their investigations to what *does* happen.

It would be the supreme irony if, when the resurrection became an acceptable possibility again, the theologians had succeeded in rejecting it! But will it ever be really acceptable?

Moral resistance

There is a moral barrier, as well as a mental one.

Why is it easier to accept the authenticity of Homer's *Iliad* than the Gospels, and that Julius Caesar invaded Britain than that Jesus rose from the dead? In both cases, the evidence is far better for the latter. However, we can believe the former without having to do anything about it. Life can go on exactly as before.

But the resurrection is quite a different matter. If Jesus rose from the dead, the claims he made for himself are valid and the claims he makes on us are equally valid. We cannot ignore him any more. We would not just have to change our minds, about him, about God, about ourselves and others; we'd have to change our morals as well. For he claimed that we are all accountable to him for how we live our lives and that he would decide our eternal destiny on this basis.

If he is right, all of us have been wrong, The implications are both profound and practical. Wanting to ignore Jesus is just a symptom of our desire to be independent of God himself – a rebellious attitude as old as the garden of Eden. If Jesus is risen, then *"Jesus is Lord"* (the oldest Christian creed). All authority in heaven and on earth has been given to him (Matthew 28:18), including the right to govern your life and mine.

Behind the reluctance to believe the evidence for the resurrection lies the reluctance to face its significance. People would rather believe it is false. They want to live life their way, not his.

So the claim that Jesus is still alive is never likely to be widely acceptable – yet one day will be universally accepted!

For there is yet another resurrection appearance still to come.

It will be seen by the whole world. The same Jesus who foretold his death, burial, resurrection and ascension in such detail also predicted that one day he would return to this earth. The New Testament mentions this future event over three hundred times. All its authors were convinced of it. If Jesus was proved right about his return from death, he will be proved right about his return to earth.

The Bible looks forward to the day when every knee will bow to him and every tongue will confess him as Lord (Philippians 2:10, quoting Isaiah 45:23). When they see his glorious body, still with its scars on hands, feet, side, back and head, they will be convinced of the truth of the resurrection. How foolish will those feel who have dismissed, denied or demythologized this mighty act of God.

But it will be too late for them to believe it or benefit from it. It is not faith when you have no choice but to accept it. Jesus' first coming was to save, but his second coming is to "judge the living and the dead" (as the Apostles' Creed puts it), to *"punish those who do not know God and do not obey the gospel"* (2 Thessalonians 1:8).

He is coming for those who have already believed in him, experienced the power of his resurrection and are looking forward to receiving a new body and living in the new heaven and earth.

May you be among that number, when the saints go marching in.

"Blessed are those who have not seen and yet have believed."
(John 20:29)